Rabindranath Tagore – The Crescent Moon

Poetry is a fascinating use of language. With almost a million words at its command it is not surprising that these Isles have produced some of the most beautiful, moving and descriptive verse through the centuries. In this series we look at individual poets who have shaped and influenced their craft and cement their place in our heritage.

In this volume we venture to the East. To met a poet who speaks a common language of love and mysticism which continues to convey valuable insights into universal themes in contemporary society.

Rabindranath Tagore (1861-1941) who was a gifted Bengali Renaissance man, distinguishing himself as a philosopher, social and political reformer and a popular author in all literary genres. He was instrumental in an increased freedom for the press and influenced Gandhi and the founders of modern India.

He composed hundreds of songs which are still sung today as they include the Indian and Bangladesh's national anthems.

His prolific literary life has left a legacy of quality novels, essays and in this collection of prose poetry some of his finest poetical works. Together they earned him the distinction of being the first Asian writer to receive the Nobel Prize in Literature in 1913.

Many of other poems are also available as an audiobook from our sister company Portable Poetry. Many samples are at our youtube channel http://www.youtube.com/user/PortablePoetry?feature=mhee   The full volume can be purchased from iTunes, Amazon and other digital stores. Among our readers are Shyama Perera Mitchley and Ghizela Rowe

Index Of Titles
THE HOME
ON THE SEASHORE
THE SOURCE
BABY'S WAY
THE UNHEEDED PAGEANT
SLEEP-STEALER
THE BEGINNING
BABY'S WORLD
WHEN AND WHY
DEFAMATION
THE JUDGE
PLAYTHINGS
THE ASTRONOMER
CLOUDS AND WAVES
THE CHAMPA FLOWER
FAIRYLAND

THE LAND OF THE EXILE
THE RAINY DAY
PAPER BOATS
THE SAILOR
THE FURTHER BANK
THE FLOWER-SCHOOL
THE MERCHANT
SYMPATHY
VOCATION
SUPERIOR
THE LITTLE BIG MAN
TWELVE O'CLOCK
AUTHORSHIP
THE WICKED POSTMAN
THE HERO
THE END
THE RECALL
THE FIRST JASMINES
THE BANYAN TREE
BENEDICTION
THE GIFT
MY SONG
THE CHILD-ANGEL
THE LAST BARGAIN
RABINDRANATH TAGORE – A Biography

THE HOME

I paced alone on the road across the field while the sunset was hiding its last gold like a miser.

The daylight sank deeper and deeper into the darkness, and the widowed land, whose harvest had been reaped, lay silent.
Suddenly a boy's shrill voice rose into the sky. He traversed the dark unseen, leaving the track of his song across the hush of the evening.

His village home lay there at the end of the waste land, beyond the sugar-cane field, hidden among the shadows of the banana and the slender areca palm, the cocoa-nut and the dark green jack-fruit trees.

I stopped for a moment in my lonely way under the starlight, and saw spread before me the darkened earth surrounding with her arms countless homes furnished with cradles and beds, mothers' hearts and evening lamps, and young lives glad with a gladness that knows nothing of its value for the world.

ON THE SEASHORE
On the seashore of endless worlds children meet.
The infinite sky is motionless overhead and the restless water is boisterous. On the seashore of endless worlds the children meet with shouts and dances.

They build their houses with sand, and they play with empty shells. With withered leaves they weave their boats and smilingly float them on the vast deep. Children have their play on the seashore of worlds.

They know not how to swim, they know not how to cast nets. Pearl-fishers dive for pearls, merchants sail in their ships, while children gather pebbles and scatter them again. They seek not for hidden treasures, they know not how to cast nets.

The sea surges up with laughter, and pale gleams the smile of the sea-beach. Death-dealing waves sing meaningless ballads to the children, even like a mother while rocking her baby's cradle. The sea plays with children, and pale gleams the smile of the sea-beach.

On the seashore of endless worlds children meet. Tempest roams in the pathless sky, ships are wrecked in the trackless water, death is abroad and children play. On the seashore of endless worlds is the great meeting of children.

THE SOURCE
The sleep that flits on baby's eyes, does anybody know from where it comes? Yes, there is a rumour that it has its dwelling where, in the fairy village among shadows of the forest dimly lit with glow-worms, there hang two shy buds of enchantment. From there it comes to kiss baby's eyes.

The smile that flickers on baby's lips when he sleeps, does anybody know where it was born? Yes, there is a rumour that a young pale beam of a crescent moon touched the edge of a vanishing autumn cloud, and there the smile was first born in the dream of a dew-washed morning, the smile that flickers on baby's lips when he sleeps.

The sweet, soft freshness that blooms on baby's limbs, does anybody know where it was hidden so long? Yes, when the mother was a young girl it lay pervading her heart in tender and silent mystery of love, the sweet, soft freshness that has bloomed on baby's limbs.

BABY'S WAY

If baby only wanted to, he could fly up to heaven this moment.
It is not for nothing that he does not leave us.
He loves to rest his head on mother's bosom, and cannot ever bear to lose sight of her.

Baby knows all manner of wise words, though few on earth can understand their meaning.
It is not for nothing that he never wants to speak.
The one thing he wants is to learn mother's words from mother's lips.
That is why he looks so innocent.

Baby had a heap of gold and pearls, yet he came like a beggar on to this earth.
It is not for nothing he came in such a disguise.
This dear little naked mendicant pretends to be utterly helpless, so that he may beg for mother's wealth of love.

Baby was so free from every tie in the land of the tiny crescent moon.
It was not for nothing he gave up his freedom.
He knows that there is room for endless joy in mother's little corner of a heart, and it is sweeter far than liberty to be caught and pressed in her dear arms.

Baby never knew how to cry. He dwelt in the land of perfect bliss.
It is not for nothing he has chosen to shed tears.
Though with the smile of his dear face he draws mother's yearning heart to him, yet his little cries over tiny troubles weave the double bond of pity and love.

THE UNHEEDED PAGEANT
Ah, who was it coloured that little frock, my child, and covered your sweet limbs with that little red tunic?
You have come out in the morning to play in the courtyard, tottering and tumbling as you run.
But who was it coloured that little frock, my child?

What is it makes you laugh, my little life-bud?
Mother smiles at you standing on the threshold.
She claps her hands and her bracelets jingle, and you dance with your bamboo stick in your hand like a tiny little shepherd.
But what is it makes you laugh, my little life-bud?

O beggar, what do you beg for, clinging to your mother's neck with both your hands?
O greedy heart, shall I pluck the world like a fruit from the sky to place it on your little rosy palm?

O beggar, what are you begging for?
The wind carries away in glee the tinkling of your anklet bells.
The sun smiles and watches your toilet. The sky watches over you when you sleep in your mother's arms, and the morning comes tiptoe to your bed and kisses your eyes.
The wind carries away in glee the tinkling of your anklet bells.

The fairy mistress of dreams is coming towards you, flying through the twilight sky.
The world-mother keeps her seat by you in your mother's heart.

He who plays his music to the stars is standing at your window with his flute.
And the fairy mistress of dreams is coming towards you, flying through the twilight sky.

SLEEP-STEALER
Who stole sleep from baby's eyes? I must know.
Clasping her pitcher to her waist mother went to fetch water from the village near by.

It was noon. The children's playtime was over; the ducks in the pond were silent.

The shepherd boy lay asleep under the shadow of the *banyan* tree.

The crane stood grave and still in the swamp near the mango grove.

In the meanwhile the Sleep-stealer came and, snatching sleep from baby's eyes, flew away.

When mother came back she found baby travelling the room over on all fours.

Who stole sleep from our baby's eyes? I must know. I must find her and chain her up.

I must look into that dark cave, where, through boulders and scowling stones, trickles a tiny stream.

I must search in the drowsy shade of the *bakula* grove, where pigeons coo in their corner, and fairies' anklets tinkle in the stillness of starry nights.

In the evening I will peep into the whispering silence of the bamboo forest, where fireflies squander their light, and will ask every creature I meet, "Can anybody tell me where the Sleep-stealer lives?"

Who stole sleep from baby's eyes? I must know.
Shouldn't I give her a good lesson if I could only catch her!

I would raid her nest and see where she hoards all her stolen sleep.

I would plunder it all, and carry it home.
I would bind her two wings securely, set her on the bank of the river, and then let her play at fishing with a reed among the rushes and water-lilies.

When the marketing is over in the evening, and the village children sit in their mothers' laps, then the night birds will mockingly din her ears with: "Whose sleep will you steal now?"

THE BEGINNING
"Where have I come from, where did you pick me up?" the baby asked its mother.
She answered half crying, half laughing, and clasping the baby to her breast, "You were hidden in my heart as its desire, my darling.

You were in the dolls of my childhood's games; and when with clay I made the image of my god every morning, I made and unmade you then. You were enshrined with our household deity, in his worship I worshipped you.

In all my hopes and my loves, in my life, in the life of my mother you have lived.
In the lap of the deathless Spirit who rules our home you have been nursed for ages.

When in girlhood my heart was opening its petals, you hovered as a fragrance about it.
Your tender softness bloomed in my youthful limbs, like a glow in the sky before the sunrise.

Heaven's first darling, twin-born with the morning light, you have floated down the stream of the world's life, and at last you have stranded on my heart.

As I gaze on your face, mystery overwhelms me; you who belong to all have become mine.
For fear of losing you I hold you tight to my breast. What magic has snared the world's treasure in these slender arms of mine?"

BABY'S WORLD
I wish I could take a quiet corner in the heart of my baby's very own world.
I know it has stars that talk to him, and a sky that stoops down to his face to amuse him with its silly clouds and rainbows.
Those who make believe to be dumb, and look as if they never could move, come creeping to his window with their stories and with trays crowded with bright toys.
I wish I could travel by the road that crosses baby's mind, and out beyond all bounds;
Where messengers run errands for no cause between the kingdoms of kings of no history;
Where Reason makes kites of her laws and flies them, and Truth sets Fact free from its fetters.

WHEN AND WHY
When I bring you coloured toys, my child, I understand why there is such a play of colours on clouds, on water, and why flowers are painted in tints, when I give coloured toys to you, my child.

When I sing to make you dance, I truly know why there is music in leaves, and why waves send their chorus of voices to the heart of the listening earth, when I sing to make you dance.

When I bring sweet things to your greedy hands, I know why there is honey in the cup of the flower, and why fruits are secretly filled with sweet juice, when I bring sweet things to your greedy hands.

When I kiss your face to make you smile, my darling, I surely understand what pleasure streams from the sky in morning light, and what delight the summer breeze brings to my body, when I kiss you to make you smile.

DEFAMATION
Why are those tears in your eyes, my child?
How horrid of them to be always scolding you for nothing?
You have stained your fingers and face with ink while writing,
is that why they call you dirty?
O, fie! Would they dare to call the full moon dirty because it has smudged its face with ink?

For every little trifle they blame you, my child. They are ready to find fault for nothing.
You tore your clothes while playing, is that why they call you untidy?
O, fie! What would they call an autumn morning that smiles through its ragged clouds?

Take no heed of what they say to you, my child.
Take no heed of what they say to you, my child.
They make a long list of your misdeeds. Everybody knows how you love sweet things, is that why they call you greedy?
O, fie! What then would they call us who love you?

THE JUDGE
Say of him what you please, but I know my child's failings.
I do not love him because he is good, but because he is my little child.

How should you know how dear he can be when you try to weigh his merits against his faults?
When I must punish him he becomes all the more a part of my being.

When I cause his tears to come my heart weeps with him.
I alone have a right to blame and punish, for he only may chastise who loves.

PLAYTHINGS
Child, how happy you are sitting in the dust, playing with a broken twig all the morning.
I smile at your play with that little bit of a broken twig.
I am busy with my accounts, adding up figures by the hour.
Perhaps you glance at me and think, "What a stupid game to spoil your morning with!"
Child, I have forgotten the art of being absorbed in sticks and mud-pies.
I seek out costly playthings, and gather lumps of gold and silver.
With whatever you find you create your glad games, I spend both my time and my strength over things I never can obtain.
In my frail canoe I struggle to cross the sea of desire, and forget that I too am playing a game.

THE ASTRONOMER
I only said, "When in the evening the round full moon gets entangled among the branches of that *Kadam* tree, couldn't somebody catch it?"

But dâdâ laughed at me and said, "Baby, you are the silliest child I have ever known. The moon is ever so far from us, how could anybody catch it?"

I said, "Dâdâ how foolish you are! When mother looks out of her window and smiles down at us playing, would you call her far away?"

Still said, "You are a stupid child! But, baby, where could you find a net big enough to catch the moon with?"
I said, "Surely you could catch it with your hands."

But dâdâ laughed and said, "You are the silliest child I have known. If it came nearer, you would see how big the moon is."

I said, "Dâdâ, what nonsense they teach at your school! When mother bends her face down to kiss us does her face look very big?"

But still dâdâ says, "You are a stupid child."

CLOUDS AND WAVES
Mother, the folk who live up in the clouds call out to me
"We play from the time we wake till the day ends.
We play with the golden dawn, we play with the silver moon.
I ask, "But, how am I to get up to you?"
They answer, "Come to the edge of the earth, lift up your hands to the sky, and you will be taken up into the clouds."
"My mother is waiting for me at home," I say. "How can I leave her and come?"
Then they smile and float away.
But I know a nicer game than that, mother.
I shall be the cloud and you the moon.
I shall cover you with both my hands, and our house-top will be the blue sky.
The folk who live in the waves call out to me
"We sing from morning till night; on and on we travel and know not where we pass."
I ask, "But, how am I to join you?" They tell me, "Come to the edge of the shore and stand with your eyes tight shut, and you will be carried out upon the waves."
I say, "My mother always wants me at home in the evening, how can I leave her and go?"
Then they smile, dance and pass by.
But I know a better game than that.
I will be the waves and you will be a strange shore.
I shall roll on and on and on, and break upon your lap with laughter.
And no one in the world will know where we both are.

THE CHAMPA FLOWER
Supposing I became a *champa* flower, just for fun, and grew on a branch high up that tree, and shook in the wind with laughter and danced upon the newly budded leaves, would you know me, mother?
You would call, "Baby, where are you?" and I should laugh to myself and keep quite quiet.
I should slyly open my petals and watch you at your work.
When after your bath, with wet hair spread on your shoulders, you walked through the shadow of the *champa* tree to the little court where you say your prayers, you would notice the scent of the flower, but not know that it came from me.
When after the midday meal you sat at the window
reading *Ramayana,* and the tree's shadow fell over your hair and your lap, I should fling my wee little shadow on to the page of your book, just where you were reading.
But would you guess that it was the tiny shadow of your little child?
When in the evening you went to the cow-shed with the lighted lamp in your hand, I should suddenly drop on to the earth again and be your own baby once more, and beg you to tell me a story.
"Where have you been, you naughty child?"
"I won't tell you, mother." That's what you and I would say then.

FAIRYLAND
If people came to know where my king's palace is, it would vanish into the air.
The walls are of white silver and the roof of shining gold.
The queen lives in a palace with seven courtyards, and she wears a jewel that cost all the wealth of seven kingdoms.
But let me tell you, mother, in a whisper, where my king's palace is.
It is at the corner of our terrace where the pot of the *tulsi* plant stands.

The princess lies sleeping on the far-away shore of the seven impassable seas.
There is none in the world who can find her but myself.

She has bracelets on her arms and pearl drops in her ears; her hair sweeps down upon the floor.
She will wake when I touch her with my magic wand, and jewels will fall from her lips when she smiles.
But let me whisper in your ear, mother; she is there in the corner of our terrace where the pot of the *tulsi* plant stands.

When it is time for you to go to the river for your bath, step up to that terrace on the roof.
I sit in the corner where the shadows of the walls meet together.
Only puss is allowed to come with me, for she knows where the barber in the story lives.
But let me whisper, mother, in your ear where the barber in the story lives.
It is at the corner of the terrace where the pot of the *tulsi* plant stands.

THE LAND OF THE EXILE
Mother, the light has grown grey in the sky; I do not know what the time is.
There is no fun in my play, so I have come to you. It is Saturday, our holiday.
Leave off your work, mother; sit here by the window and tell me where the desert of Tepântar in the fairy tale is?

The shadow of the rains has covered the day from end to end.
The fierce lightning is scratching the sky with its nails.
When the clouds rumble and it thunders, I love to be afraid in my heart and cling to you.
When the heavy rain patters for hours on the bamboo leaves, and our windows shake and rattle at the gusts of wind, I like to sit alone in the room, mother, with you, and hear you talk about the desert of Tepântar in the fairy tale.

Where is it, mother, on the shore of what sea, at the foot of what hills, in the kingdom of what king?
There are no hedges there to mark the fields, no footpath across it by which the villagers reach their village in the evening, or the woman who gathers dry sticks in the forest can bring her load to the market. With patches of yellow grass in the sand and only one tree where the pair of wise old birds have their nest, lies the desert of Tepântar.

I can imagine how, on just such a cloudy day, the young son of the king is riding alone on a grey horse through the desert, in search of the princess who lies imprisoned in the giant's palace across that unknown water.

When the haze of the rain comes down in the distant sky, and lightning starts up like a sudden fit of pain, does he remember his unhappy mother, abandoned by the king, sweeping the cow-stall and wiping her eyes, while he rides through the desert of Tepântar in the fairy tale?

See, mother, it is almost dark before the day is over, and there are no travellers yonder on the village road.

The shepherd boy has gone home early from the pasture, and men have left their fields to sit on mats under the eaves of their huts, watching the scowling clouds.

Mother, I have left all my books on the shelf--do not ask me to do my lessons now.

When I grow up and am big like my father, I shall learn all that must be learnt.

But just for to-day, tell me, mother, where the desert of Tepântar in the fairy tale is?

THE RAINY DAY

Sullen clouds are gathering fast over the black fringe of the forest.

O child, do not go out!

The palm trees in a row by the lake are smiting their heads against the dismal sky; the crows with their draggled wings are silent on the tamarind branches, and the eastern bank of the river is haunted by a deepening gloom.

Our cow is lowing loud, tied at the fence.

O child, wait here till I bring her into the stall.

Men have crowded into the flooded field to catch the fishes as they escape from the overflowing ponds; the rain water is running in rills through the narrow lanes like a laughingboy who has run away from his mother to tease her.

Listen, someone is shouting for the boatman at the ford.

O child, the daylight is dim, and the crossing at the ferry is closed.
The sky seems to ride fast upon the madly-rushing rain; the water in the river is loud and impatient; women have hastened home early from the Ganges with their filled pitchers.

The evening lamps must be made ready.
O child, do not go out!
The road to the market is desolate, the lane to the river is slippery. The wind is roaring and struggling among the bamboo branches like a wild beast tangled in a net.

PAPER BOATS
Day by day I float my paper boats one by one down the running stream.
In big black letters I write my name on them and the name of the village where I live.
I hope that someone in some strange land will find them and know who I am.
I load my little boats with *shiuli* flowers from our garden, and hope that these blooms of the dawn will be carried safely to land in the night.
I launch my paper boats and look up into the sky and see the little clouds setting their white bulging sails.
I know not what playmate of mine in the sky sends them down the air to race with my boats!
When night comes I bury my face in my arms and dream that my paper boats float on and on under the midnight stars.
The fairies of sleep are sailing in them, and the lading is their baskets full of dreams.

THE SAILOR
The boat of the boatman Madhu is moored at the wharf of Rajgunj.
It is uselessly laden with jute, and has been lying there idle for ever so long.
If he would only lend me his boat, I should man her with a hundred oars, and hoist sails, five or six or seven.

I should never steer her to stupid markets. I should sail the seven seas and the thirteen rivers of fairyland.

But, mother, you won't weep for me in a corner.
I am not going into the forest like Ramachandra to come back only after fourteen years.
I shall become the prince of the story, and fill my boat with whatever I like.
I shall take my friend Ashu with me. We shall sail merrily across the seven seas and the thirteen rivers of fairyland.

We shall set sail in the early morning light.
When at noontide you are bathing at the pond, we shall be in the land of a strange king.
We shall pass the ford of Tirpurni, and leave behind us the desert of Tepântar.
When we come back it will be getting dark, and I shall tell you of all that we have seen.
I shall cross the seven seas and the thirteen rivers of fairyland.

THE FURTHER BANK
I long to go over there to the further bank of the river,
Where those boats are tied to the bamboo poles in a line;
Where men cross over in their boats in the morning with ploughs on their shoulders to till their far-away fields;
Where the cowherds make their lowing cattle swim across to the riverside pasture;
Whence they all come back home in the evening, leaving the jackals to howl in the island overgrown with weeds,
Mother, if you don't mind, I should like to become the boatman of the ferry when I am grown up.

They say there are strange pools hidden behind that high bank,
Where flocks of wild ducks come when the rains are over, and thick reeds grow round the margins where waterbirds lay their eggs;
Where snipes with their dancing tails stamp their tiny footprints upon the clean soft mud;
Where in the evening the tall grasses crested with white flowers invite the moonbeam to float upon their waves.
Mother, if you don't mind, I should like to become the boatman of the ferryboat when I am grown up.

I shall cross and cross back from bank to bank, and all the boys and girls of the village will wonder at me while they are bathing.
When the sun climbs the mid sky and morning wears on to noon, I shall come running to you, saying, "Mother, I am hungry!"
When the day is done and the shadows cower under the trees, I shall come back in the dusk.
I shall never go away from you into the town to work like father.
Mother, if you don't mind, I should like to become the boatman of the ferryboat when I am grown up.

THE FLOWER-SCHOOL
When storm clouds rumble in the sky and June showers come down,
The moist east wind comes marching over the heath to blow its bagpipes among the bamboos.
Then crowds of flowers come out of a sudden, from nobody knows where, and dance upon the grass in wild glee.

Mother, I really think the flowers go to school underground.
They do their lessons with doors shut, and if they want to come out to play before it is time, their master makes them stand in a corner.

When the rains come they have their holidays.
Branches clash together in the forest, and the leaves rustle in the wild wind, the thunder-clouds clap their giant hands and the flower children rush out in dresses of pink and yellow and white.

Do you know, mother, their home is in the sky, where the stars are.
Haven't you seen how eager they are to get there? Don't you know why they are in such a hurry?
Of course, I can guess to whom they raise their arms: they have their mother as I have my own.

THE MERCHANT
Imagine, mother, that you are to stay at home and I am to travel into strange lands.
Imagine that my boat is ready at the landing fully laden.
Now think well, mother, before you say what I shall bring for you when I come back.

Mother, do you want heaps and heaps of gold?
There, by the banks of golden streams, fields are full of golden harvest.
And in the shade of the forest path the golden *champa* flowers drop on the ground.
I will gather them all for you in many hundred baskets.

Mother, do you want pearls big as the raindrops of autumn?
I shall cross to the pearl island shore. There in the early morning light pearls tremble on the meadow flowers, pearls drop on the grass, and pearls are scattered on the sand in spray by the wild sea-waves.
My brother shall have a pair of horses with wings to fly among the clouds. For father I shall bring a magic pen that, without his knowing, will write of itself.
For you, mother, I must have the casket and jewel that cost seven kings their kingdoms.

SYMPATHY
If I were only a little puppy, not your baby, mother dear, would you say "No" to me if I tried to eat from your dish?
Would you drive me off, saying to me, "Get away, you naughty little puppy?"
Then go, mother, go! I will never come to you when you call me, and never let you feed me any more.
If I were only a little green parrot, and not your baby, mother dear, would you keep me chained lest I should fly away?
Would you shake your finger at me and say, "What an ungrateful wretch of a bird! It is gnawing at its chain day and night?"
Then, go, mother, go! I will run away into the woods; I will never let you take me in your arms again.

VOCATION
WHEN the gong sounds ten in the morning and I walk to school by our lane,
Every day I meet the hawker crying, "Bangles, crystal bangles!"
There is nothing to hurry him on, there is no road he must take, no place he must go to, no time when he must come home.
I wish I were a hawker, spending my day in the road, crying, "Bangles, crystal bangles!"

When at four in the afternoon I come back from the school,
I can see through the gate of that house the gardener digging the ground.
He does what he likes with his spade, he soils his clothes with dust, nobody takes him to task if he gets baked in the sun or gets wet.
I wish I were a gardener digging away at the garden with nobody to stop me from digging.

Just as it gets dark in the evening and my mother sends me to bed,
I can see through my open window the watchman walking up and down.
The lane is dark and lonely, and the street-lamp stands like a giant with one red eye in its head.

The watchman swings his lantern and walks with his shadow at his side, and never once goes to bed in his life.
I wish I were a watchman walking the streets all night, chasing the shadows with my lantern.

SUPERIOR
Mother, your baby is silly! She is so absurdly childish!
She does not know the difference between the lights in the streets and the stars.
When we play at eating with pebbles, she thinks they are real food, and tries to put them into her mouth.
When I open a book before her and ask her to learn her a, b, c, she tears the leaves with her hands and roars for joy at nothing; this is your baby's way of doing her lesson.
When I shake my head at her in anger and scold her and call her naughty, she laughs and thinks it great fun.
Everybody knows that father is away, but if in play I call aloud "Father," she looks about her in excitement and thinks that father is near.
When I hold my class with the donkeys that our washerman brings to carry away the clothes and I warn her that I am the schoolmaster, she will scream for no reason and call me dâdâ.
Your baby wants to catch the moon. She is so funny; she calls Ganesh Gânush.
Mother, your baby is silly, she is so absurdly childish!

THE LITTLE BIG MAN
I am small because I am a little child. I shall be big when I am as old as my father is.
My teacher will come and say, "It is late, bring your slate and your books."
I shall tell him, "Do you not know I am as big as father? And I must not have lessons any more."
My master will wonder and say, "He can leave his books if he likes, for he is grown up."

I shall dress myself and walk to the fair where the crowd is thick.
My uncle will come rushing up to me and say, "You will get lost, my boy; let me carry you."
I shall answer, "Can't you see, uncle, I am as big as father. I must go to the fair alone."
Uncle will say, "Yes, he can go wherever he likes, for he is grown up."

Mother will come from her bath when I am giving money to my nurse, for I shall know how to open the box with my key.
Mother will say, "What are you about, naughty child?"

I shall tell her, "Mother, don't you know, I am as big as father, and I must give silver to my nurse."
Mother will say to herself, "He can give money to whom he likes, for he is grown up."

In the holiday time in October father will come home and, thinking that I am still a baby, will bring for me from the town little shoes and small silken frocks.
I shall say, "Father, give them to my dâdâ [*elder brother*], for I am as big as you are."
Father will think and say, "He can buy his own clothes if he likes, for he is grown up."

TWELVE O'CLOCK
Mother, I do want to leave off my lessons now. I have been at my book all the morning.
You say it is only twelve o'clock. Suppose it isn't any later; can't you ever think it is afternoon when it is only twelve o'clock?
I can easily imagine now that the sun has reached the edge of that rice-field, and the old fisher-woman is gathering herbs for her supper by the side of the pond.
I can just shut my eyes and think that the shadows are growing darker under the *madar*tree, and the water in the pond looks shiny black.
If twelve o'clock can come in the night, why can't the night come when it is twelve o'clock?

AUTHORSHIP
You say that father writes a lot of books, but what he writes I don't understand.
He was reading to you all the evening, but could you really make out what he meant?
What nice stories, mother, you can tell us! Why can't father write like that, I wonder?
Did he never hear from his own mother stories of giants and fairies and princesses?
Has he forgotten them all?

Often when he gets late for his bath you have to go and call him an hundred times.
You wait and keep his dishes warm for him, but he goes on writing and forgets.
Father always plays at making books.
If ever I go to play in father's room, you come and call me, "what a naughty child!"

If I make the slightest noise, you say, "Don't you see that father's at his work?"
What's the fun of always writing and writing?

When I take up father's pen or pencil and write upon his book just as he does, a, b, c, d, e, f, g, h, i, why do you get cross with me, then, mother? You never say a word when father writes.

When my father wastes such heaps of paper, mother, you don't seem to mind at all.
But if I take only one sheet to make a boat with, you say, "Child, how troublesome you are!"
What do you think of father's spoiling sheets and sheets of paper with black marks all over on both sides?

THE WICKED POSTMAN
Why do you sit there on the floor so quiet and silent, tell me, mother dear?
The rain is coming in through the open window, making you all wet, and you don't mind it.
Do you hear the gong striking four? It is time for my brother to come home from school.
What has happened to you that you look so strange?
Haven't you got a letter from father to-day?
I saw the postman bringing letters in his bag for almost everybody in the town.
Only, father's letters he keeps to read himself. I am sure the postman is a wicked man.
But don't be unhappy about that, mother dear.
To-morrow is market day in the next village. You ask your maid to buy some pens and papers.
I myself will write all father's letters; you will not find a single mistake.
I shall write from A right up to K.
But, mother, why do you smile?
You don't believe that I can write as nicely as father does!
But I shall rule my paper carefully, and write all the letters beautifully big.
When I finish my writing, do you think I shall be so foolish as father and drop it into the horrid postman's bag?
I shall bring it to you myself without waiting, and letter by letter help you to read my writing.
I know the postman does not like to give you the really nice letters.

THE HERO
Mother, let us imagine we are travelling, and passing through a strange and dangerous country.

You are riding in a palanquin and I am trotting by you on a red horse.
It is evening and the sun goes down. The waste of *Joradighi* lies wan and grey before us. The land is desolate and barren.
You are frightened and thinking "I know not where we have come to."
I say to you, "Mother, do not be afraid."

The meadow is prickly with spiky grass, and through it runs a narrow broken path.
There are no cattle to be seen in the wide field; they have gone to their village stalls.
It grows dark and dim on the land and sky, and we cannot tell where we are going.
Suddenly you call me and ask me in a whisper, "What light is that near the bank?"

Just then there bursts out a fearful yell, and figures come running towards us.
You sit crouched in your palanquin and repeat the names of the gods in prayer.
The bearers, shaking in terror, hide themselves in the thorny bush.
I shout to you, "Don't be afraid, mother. I am here."

With long sticks in their hands and hair all wild about their heads, they come nearer and nearer.
I shout, "Have a care! you villains! One step more and you are dead men."
They give another terrible yell and rush forward.
You clutch my hand and say, "Dear boy, for heaven's sake, keep away from them."
I say, "Mother, just you watch me."

Then I spur my horse for a wild gallop, and my sword and buckler clash against each other.
The fight becomes so fearful, mother, that it would give you a cold shudder could you see it from your palanquin.
Many of them fly, and a great number are cut to pieces.
I know you are thinking, sitting all by yourself, that your boy must be dead by this time.
But I come to you all stained with blood, and say, "Mother, the fight is over now."
You come out and kiss me, pressing me to your heart, and you say to yourself,
"I don't know what I should do if I hadn't my boy to escort me."
A thousand useless things happen day after day, and why couldn't such a thing come true by chance?
It would be like a story in a book.

My brother would say, "Is it possible? I always thought he was so delicate!"
Our village people would all say in amazement, "Was it not lucky that the boy was with his mother?"

THE END
It is time for me to go, mother; I am going.
When in the paling darkness of the lonely dawn you stretch out your arms for your baby in the bed, I shall say, "Baby is not there!"--mother, I am going.
I shall become a delicate draught of air and caress you; and I shall be ripples in the water when you bathe, and kiss you and kiss you again.
In the gusty night when the rain patters on the leaves you will hear my whisper in your bed, and my laughter will flash with the lightning through the open window into your room.
If you lie awake, thinking of your baby till late into the night, I shall sing to you from the stars, "Sleep mother, sleep."
On the straying moonbeams I shall steal over your bed, and lie upon your bosom while you sleep.
I shall become a dream, and through the little opening of your eyelids I shall slip into the depths of your sleep; and when you wake up and look round startled, like a twinkling firefly I shall flit out into the darkness.
When, on the great festival of *puja,* the neighbours' children come and play about the house, I shall melt into the music of the flute and throb in your heart all day.
Dear auntie will come with *puja*-presents and will ask, "Where is our baby, sister? Mother, you will tell her softly, "He is in the pupils of my eyes, he is in my body and in my soul."

THE RECALL
The night was dark when she went away, and they slept.
The night is dark now, and I call for her, "Come back, my darling; the world is asleep; and no one would know, if you came for a moment while stars are gazing at stars."

She went away when the trees were in bud and the spring was young.
Now the flowers are in high bloom and I call, "Come back, my darling. The children gather and scatter flowers in reckless sport. And if you come and take one little blossom no one will miss it."

Those that used to play are playing still, so spendthrift is life.
I listen to their chatter and call, "Come back, my darling, for mother's heart is full to the brim with love, and if you come to snatch only one little kiss from her no one will grudge it."

THE FIRST JASMINES
Ah, these jasmines, these white jasmines!
I seem to remember the first day when I filled my hands with these jasmines, these white jasmines.
I have loved the sunlight, the sky and the green earth;
I have heard the liquid murmur of the river through the darkness of midnight;
Autumn sunsets have come to me at the bend of a road in the lonely waste, like a bride raising her veil to accept her lover.
Yet my memory is still sweet with the first white jasmines that I held in my hand when I was a child.

Many a glad day has come in my life, and I have laughed with merrymakers on festival nights.
On grey mornings of rain I have crooned many an idle song.
I have worn round my neck the evening wreath of *bakulas* woven by the hand of love.
Yet my heart is sweet with the memory of the first fresh jasmines that filled my hands when I was a child.

THE BANYAN TREE
O you shaggy-headed banyan tree standing on the bank of the pond, have you forgotten the little child, like the birds that have nested in your branches and left you?
Do you not remember how he sat at the window and wondered at the tangle of your roots that plunged underground?
The women would come to fill their jars in the pond, and your huge black shadow would wriggle on the water like sleep struggling to wake up.
Sunlight danced on the ripples like restless tiny shuttles weaving golden tapestry.
Two ducks swam by the weedy margin above their shadows, and the child would sit still and think.
He longed to be the wind and blow through your rustling branches, to be your shadow and lengthen with the day on the water, to be a bird and perch on your top-most twig, and to float like those ducks among the weeds and shadows.

BENEDICTION
Bless this little heart, this white soul that has won the kiss of heaven for our earth.
He loves the light of the sun, he loves the sight of his mother's face.
He has not learned to despise the dust, and to hanker after gold.

Clasp him to your heart and bless him.
He has come into this land of an hundred cross-roads.
I know not how he chose you from the crowd, came to your door, and grasped your hand to ask his way.
He will follow you, laughing and talking, and not a doubt in his heart.
Keep his trust, lead him straight and bless him.
Lay your hand on his head, and pray that though the waves underneath grow threatening, yet the breath from above may come and fill his sails and waft him to the haven of peace.
Forget him not in your hurry, let him come to your heart and bless him.

THE GIFT
I want to give you something, my child, for we are drifting in the stream of the world.
Our lives will be carried apart, and our love forgotten.
But I am not so foolish as to hope that I could buy your heart with my gifts.
Young is your life, your path long, and you drink the love we bring you at one draught and turn and run away from us.
You have your play and your playmates. What harm is there if you have no time or thought for us.
We, indeed, have leisure enough in old age to count the days that are past, to cherish in our hearts what our hands have lost for ever.
The river runs swift with a song, breaking through all barriers. But the mountain stays and remembers, and follows her with his love.

MY SONG
This song of mine will wind its music around you, my child, like the fond arms of love.
This song of mine will touch your forehead like a kiss of blessing.
When you are alone it will sit by your side and whisper in your ear, when you are in the crowd it will fence you about with aloofness.
My song will be like a pair of wings to your dreams, it will transport your heart to the verge of the unknown.
It will be like the faithful star overhead when dark night is over your road.
My song will sit inthe pupils of your eyes, and will carry your sight into the heart of things.
And when my voice is silent in death, my song will speak in your living heart.

THE CHILD-ANGEL
They clamour and fight, they doubt and despair, they know no end to their wranglings.

Let your life come amongst them like a flame of light, my child, unflickering and pure, and delight them into silence.
They are cruel in their greed and their envy, their words are like hidden knives thirsting for blood.
Go and stand amidst their scowling hearts, my child, and let your gentle eyes fall upon them like the forgiving peace of the evening over the strife of the day.
Let them see your face, my child, and thus know the meaning of all things; let them love you and thus love each other.
Come and take your seat in the bosom of the limitless, my child. At sunrise open and raise your heart like a blossoming flower, and at sunset bend your head and in silence complete the worship of the day.

THE LAST BARGAIN
"Come and hire me," I cried, while in the morning I was walking on the stone-paved road.
Sword in hand, the King came in his chariot.
He held my hand and said, "I will hire you with my power."
But his power counted for nought, and he went away in his chariot.

In the heat of the midday the houses stood with shut doors.
I wandered along the crooked lane.
An old man came out with his bag of gold.
He pondered and said, "I will hire you with my money."
He weighed his coins one by one, but I turned away.

It was evening. The garden hedge was all aflower.
The fair maid came out and said, "I will hire you with a smile."
Her smile paled and melted into tears, and she went back alone into the dark.

The sun glistened on the sand, and the sea waves broke waywardly.
A child sat playing with shells.
He raised his head and seemed to know me, and said, "I hire you with nothing."
From thenceforward that bargain struck in child's play made me a free man.

RABINDRANATH TAGORE – A Biography
Rabindranath Tagore (1861-1941) is an Indian poet, playwright, novelist, composer, painter and a national icon of his country. His profuse literary production ranges from collections of poems such as *Manasi* (1890), *Gitanjali* (1910) and Patraput (1936) to drama such as *Visarjan* (1890), *Raja* (1910), *Muktadhara* (1922) and *Chandalika* (1938) and even numerous musical compositions and songs. In addition, Tagore's

publications include a number of novels and several volumes of short stories including his widely appreciated *Gora* (1910) along with *Chaturanga* (1916) and *Ghare-Baire* (1916). The latter is one of his many works that were adapted to cinema.

Born in Calcutta, India, to a well-off family, Rabindranath Tagore was raised and educated mainly by servants. His father Devendranath Tagore is a saint and a religious leader of the Adi Dham faith and the Brahmo sect founded by the family's patriarchs. Young Rabindranath Tagore's home was animated by discussions of literary publications, arts, theatrical performances and classical music where most of his 14 siblings were much interested in arts, poetry, music, philosophy and theatre, such as his older sister, Swarnakumari Devi, the renowned Indian novelist, poet and musician.

In addition to such a supportive environment for artistic appreciation and creativity, Tagore's father made him discover language, literature, history and poetry, taking him for long journeys around the country. In 1873, they both left home for the hill station at Dalhousie. Named after the British Governor-General Lord Dalhousie who used to visit it during his summer holidays, the station is surrounded by captivating green hills and heaven-like vistas. During the months spent there, Tagore must have found in the station's assortments of Hindu art and temples, along with the European architecture of its summer residences, a magnificent blending of East and West.

Readers of Tagore's poetry, novels and short stories, such as "The Fruitseller from Kabul," to name but a sample, can surely detect in their imagery and emotional outlets the influence of Dalhousie's breath-taking sceneries and verdure. Tagore's journey with his father was mainly meant to be a necessary stage towards intellectual and moral maturity and individuation. The lessons that the father transmitted to the son in such an inspirational spot were not only meant to be informational lessons but also spiritual ones. Indeed, being a very respected spiritual figure who wished to hand on the torch to younger disciples, Tagore's father inculcated in him mystical yearnings for spiritual knowledge and existential meaning.

It is, however, noteworthy that despite his conspicuous lust for knowledge, Tagore hated the "yoke" of formal education and thought that classroom teaching could only muffle young people's innate and instinctive thirst for discovery and adventure. The two long journeys that he had with his father only reinforced this attitude as they helped nourish his love for nature and the divine. Helped by his father, his brother Hemendranath and the house servants, Tagore studied language, literature, mathematics, geography and history and practiced different sports at home and in the family's manor. When his father sent him to

London to study law in 1878, he quickly left University College London and chose to study language, literature and music by himself. Two years later, he travelled back to India without getting the formal degree he was sent for.

Tagore expressed in many an occasion his belief that teaching should arouse curiosity rather than be informative and he strove to put his ideas into practice particularly by founding the Visva-Bharati school, which has now become the Visva-Bharati University, where he established the "brahmacharya" educational system. The main characteristic of Tagore's educational conception was to have teachers incite their students to discover and learn through employing intellectual and spiritual motivational strategies.

As for his writings, Tagore was a genuine prodigy who started weaving his earliest verses by the age of eight in the family's Calcutta residence. A few years later, he pseudonymously published his first collection of poems which was an astounding success to the point that local critics thought the compilation to belong to the 17th-century poet Bhanusimha. He soon shifted to writing short stories and plays to achieve considerable fame in the region. While all his writings were in his native Bengali language, he eventually decided to address Western readers by translating some of his own works into English.

The English versions of his poetic works such as *Manasi* (1890), *Gitimalya* (1914) and mainly what is today considered in the West as his magnum opus, *Gitanjali* (1910), quickly gained ground among Western literary circles. Such works were read, reviewed and prefaced by leading literary figures of the time like William Butler Yeats and Ezra Pound. Tagore soon became an oriental icon who stands for India's literary, spiritual and cultural heritage. In 1913, the relatively small part of his works discovered by the West earned him the Nobel Prize in Literature. In 1915, he was also knighted by the British Crown for his literary achievements. Once famous in the West, Tagore toured Britain and the United States and lectured in many other European and non-European countries to meet and interact with important celebrities around the world including the celebrated German-born physicist Albert Einstein, Thomas Mann, George Bernard Shaw and H.G. Wells, among many others.

Politically, while Tagore's commitment manifested in his harsh criticism of nationalist extremism and in his avant-garde and reformatory positions at home, he denounced imperialism and advocated universalism and internationalism in the world. In India, he was known for his rejection of the culture of victimhood and for inciting his countrymen to have the courage of assuming the responsibilities of their misfortunes. He saw that salvation could only be realized through education and self-help. In addition to that, Tagore was also socially active in his homeland, supporting students and the poor. As for foreign affairs, Tagore denounced British colonialism and even renounced the honor previously granted by the British Crown in protest against the 1919 Jallianwala Bagh massacre.

Such political views were explicitly expressed in some of Tagore's writings and musical compositions, two of which were chosen by India and Bangladesh as national anthems. His friend Mahatma Gandhi, the celebrated leader of the Indian nationalist movement, expressed his appreciation of these compositions and was said to favor the "Ekla Chalo Re" hymn.

Towards the twilight of his career, Tagore developed new interests, mainly in arts, paintings and sciences. This is mainly expressed in stories like *Se* (1937) and *Tin Sangi* (1940) as well as in his collection of essays entitled *Visva-Parichay* (1937) which represents a literary man's exploration of the fields of astronomy, physics and biology. He even took up drawing and painting at a late age and organized exhibitions of his works in Paris and other cities.

Towards the end of the 1930s, old Rabindranath Tagore's health started to deteriorate until he died on August 7th, 1941, leaving a gigantic oeuvre of numerous volumes of fine poetry, hundreds of texts, short stories, novels, plays, paintings, doodles, more than two thousand songs, two autobiographies and numerous travelogues, essays and lectures. Tagore's life experience had taught him that divisions between human beings are nothing but an unpleasant mirage. Generally, his oeuvre invites and incites its readers to the exploration of the Other, the exploration of the Self. The following extract from his masterpiece *Gitanjali* may serve as a perfect illustration of Tagore's philosophical vision:

The time that my journey takes is long and the way of it long.
I came out on the chariot of the first gleam of light, and pursued my voyage through the wildernesses of worlds leaving my track on many a star and planet.

It is the most distant course that comes nearest to thyself, and that training is the most intricate which leads to the utter simplicity of a tune. The traveller has to knock at every alien door to come to his own, and one has to wander through all the outer worlds to reach the innermost shrine at the end.

My eyes strayed far and wide before I shut them and said 'Here art thou!' The question and the cry 'Oh, where?' melt into tears of a thousand streams and deluge the world with the flood of the assurance 'I am!'
(Song XII)

Rabindranath Tagore - A Biography

Rabindranath Tagore (1861-1941) is an Indian poet, playwright, novelist, composer, painter and a national icon of his country. His profuse literary production ranges from collections of poems such as *Manasi* (1890), *Gitanjali* (1910) and Patraput (1936) to drama such as *Visarjan* (1890), *Raja* (1910), *Muktadhara* (1922) and *Chandalika* (1938) and even numerous musical compositions and songs. In addition, Tagore's publications include a number of novels and several volumes of short stories including his widely appreciated *Gora* (1910) along with *Chaturanga* (1916) and *Ghare-Baire* (1916). The latter is one of his many works that were adapted to cinema.

Born in Calcutta, India, to a well-off family, Rabindranath Tagore was raised and educated mainly by servants. His father Devendranath Tagore is a saint and a religious leader of the Adi Dham faith and the Brahmo sect founded by the family's patriarchs. Young Rabindranath Tagore's home was animated by discussions of literary publications, arts, theatrical performances and classical music where most of his 14 siblings were much interested in arts, poetry, music, philosophy and theatre, such as his older sister, Swarnakumari Devi, the renowned Indian novelist, poet and musician.

In addition to such a supportive environment for artistic appreciation and creativity, Tagore's father made him discover language, literature, history and poetry, taking him for long journeys around the country. In 1873, they both left home for the hill station at Dalhousie. Named after the British Governor-General Lord Dalhousie who used to visit it during his summer holidays, the station is surrounded by captivating green hills and heaven-like vistas. During the months spent there, Tagore must have found in the station's assortments of Hindu art and temples, along with the European architecture of its summer residences, a magnificent blending of East and West.

Readers of Tagore's poetry, novels and short stories, such as "The Fruitseller from Kabul," to name but a sample, can surely detect in their imagery and emotional outlets the influence of Dalhousie's breath-taking sceneries and verdure. Tagore's journey with his father was mainly meant to be a necessary stage towards intellectual and moral maturity and individuation. The lessons that the father transmitted to the son in such an inspirational spot were not only meant to be informational lessons but also spiritual ones. Indeed, being a very respected spiritual figure who wished to hand on the torch to younger disciples, Tagore's father inculcated in him mystical yearnings for spiritual knowledge and existential meaning.

It is, however, noteworthy that despite his conspicuous lust for knowledge, Tagore hated the "yoke" of formal education and thought that classroom teaching could only muffle young people's innate and instinctive thirst for discovery and adventure. The two long journeys that he had with his father only reinforced this attitude as they helped nourish his love for nature and the divine. Helped by his father, his brother Hemendranath and the house servants, Tagore studied language, literature, mathematics, geography and history and practiced different sports at home and in the family's manor. When his father sent him to London to study law in 1878, he quickly left University College London and chose to study language, literature and music by himself. Two years later, he travelled back to India without getting the formal degree he was sent for.

Tagore expressed in many an occasion his belief that teaching should arouse curiosity rather than be informative and he strove to put his ideas into practice particularly by founding the Visva-Bharati school, which has now become the Visva-Bharati University, where he established the "brahmacharya" educational system. The main characteristic of Tagore's educational conception was to have teachers incite their students to discover and learn through employing intellectual and spiritual motivational strategies.

As for his writings, Tagore was a genuine prodigy who started weaving his earliest verses by the age of eight in the family's Calcutta residence. A few years later, he pseudonymously published his first collection of poems which was an astounding success to the point that local critics thought the compilation to belong to the 17th-century poet Bhanusimha. He soon shifted to writing short stories and plays to achieve considerable fame in the region. While all his writings were in his native Bengali language, he eventually decided to address Western readers by translating some of his own works into English.

The English versions of his poetic works such as *Manasi* (1890), *Gitimalya* (1914) and mainly what is today considered in the West as his magnum opus,

Gitanjali (1910), quickly gained ground among Western literary circles. Such works were read, reviewed and prefaced by leading literary figures of the time like William Butler Yeats and Ezra Pound. Tagore soon became an oriental icon who stands for India's literary, spiritual and cultural heritage. In 1913, the relatively small part of his works discovered by the West earned him the Nobel Prize in Literature. In 1915, he was also knighted by the British Crown for his literary achievements.

Once famous in the West, Tagore toured Britain and the United States and lectured in many other European and non-European countries to meet and interact with important celebrities around the world including the celebrated German-born physicist Albert Einstein, Thomas Mann, George Bernard Shaw and H.G. Wells, among many others.

Politically, while Tagore's commitment manifested in his harsh criticism of nationalist extremism and in his avant-garde and reformatory positions at home, he denounced imperialism and advocated universalism and internationalism in the world. In India, he was known for his rejection of the culture of victimhood and for inciting his countrymen to have the courage of assuming the responsibilities of their misfortunes. He saw that salvation could only be realized through education and self-help. In addition to that, Tagore was also socially active in his homeland, supporting students and the poor. As for foreign affairs, Tagore denounced British colonialism and even renounced the honor previously granted by the British Crown in protest against the 1919 Jallianwala Bagh massacre.

Such political views were explicitly expressed in some of Tagore's writings and musical compositions, two of which were chosen by India and Bangladesh as national anthems. His friend Mahatma Gandhi, the celebrated leader of the Indian nationalist movement, expressed his appreciation of these compositions and was said to favor the "Ekla Chalo Re" hymn.

Towards the twilight of his career, Tagore developed new interests, mainly in arts, paintings and sciences. This is mainly expressed in stories like *Se* (1937) and *Tin Sangi* (1940) as well as in his collection of essays entitled *Visva-Parichay* (1937) which represents a literary man's exploration of the fields of astronomy, physics and biology. He even took up drawing and painting at a late age and organized exhibitions of his works in Paris and other cities.

Towards the end of the 1930s, old Rabindranath Tagore's health started to deteriorate until he died on August 7th, 1941, leaving a gigantic oeuvre of numerous volumes of fine poetry, hundreds of texts, short stories, novels, plays, paintings, doodles, more than two thousand songs, two autobiographies and numerous travelogues, essays and lectures.

Tagore's life experience had taught him that divisions between human beings are nothing but an unpleasant mirage. Generally, his oeuvre invites and incites its readers to the exploration of the Other, the exploration of the Self. The following extract from his masterpiece *Gitanjali* may serve as a perfect illustration of Tagore's philosophical vision:

The time that my journey takes is long and the way of it long.
I came out on the chariot of the first gleam of light, and pursued my voyage through the wildernesses of worlds leaving my track on many a star and planet.
It is the most distant course that comes nearest to thyself, and that training is the most intricate which leads to the utter simplicity of a tune.
The traveller has to knock at every alien door to come to his own, and one has to wander through all the outer worlds to reach the innermost shrine at the end.
My eyes strayed far and wide before I shut them and said 'Here art thou!'
The question and the cry 'Oh, where?' melt into tears of a thousand streams and deluge the world with the flood of the assurance 'I am!' (Song XII)

www.ingramcontent.com/pod-product-compliance
Lightning Source LLC
Chambersburg PA
CBHW061316040426
42444CB00010B/2675